BUILD
UNIVERSES

Ekaterina Dukas

Ekphrasticon

© 2021 **Europe Books** | London
www.europebooks.co.uk – info@europebooks.co.uk

ISBN 979-12-201-0986-4
First edition: July 2021

Distribution for the United Kingdom: **Vine House Distribution ltd**

Printed for Italy by Rotomail Italia
Finito di stampare nel mese di luglio 2021
presso Rotomail Italia S.p.A. - Vignate (MI)

Ekphrasticon

*To the artists, models and heroes who inspired this pilgrimage
to the meaning and keep passionately its candle lighted.*

PART 1
PAINTING

THE RECLINING REBEL
Art, R. Indiana, USA, 1977

You can step on me
rave ravish roar –
that is your art
for art's sake
I won't shout –

I am voiceless,
but not pointless:
I can in-verse the tangent
back to front to heart
and re-throb with its branches
vaulting on different planets

Just remember –
we both hang on the same one.

###

Universal Public Domain

THE MEASURE
Democritus and Protagoras, Salvator Rosa, Naples, 1664

Dark angry storm vultures are attempting
turbulent landing forcing the sun
to express a blazing message of distress.
The blast is accelerating
against frail old Democritus
and may soon oust him and
the whole venture out of the canvas.

But his mathematical Excellency
has scooped the scheme to the last
measure and knows he has a good time
to enjoy this finding on the road:
Man, what is your name?
Are you Athenian?

How could you do that?
Protagoras is at a loss
over his bunch of sticks,
he was just rushing home
before the skies fall; instead,
 he was now supposed to unriddle
the gist of the smartest mind in the land.
He went on: *How did you determine*
the perimeter of this irregular cluster
of variable curves to calculate
such a perfect knot fixed as a verse?!
Protagoras went from loss to surprise –
he had found this old bunch
on the road and was just strapping it firm
to keep it safe from the coming storm:
This refuse is good only to be burnt –
can light an obtuse corner, a crescent of a yard,
or char a fraction of a ghost,
he thought while scanning
the master's wondering gesture.
Democritus' students excelled:
What a novel idea, may prove
a new axiom, an unknown theorem…
Or just a song - how to bundle
treasures found on the road,
how to tie them on one accord,
tune them around a mid-point,
secure them with a major rounding
closing at a new figurative finding.
The students went on:
A Eureka moment!
Once in a generation!
Lucky we!
But who could that man be?

That man never reached home,
he followed Democritus' schooling steps
and found new mathematical straps
for his bunch of sophist knacks
to be able to tie, fix and verse it along
wherever his mind went on,
until one night he went out of his mind -
and burnt it to cinders-
to see through the ghosts' sifting wings that
Man is the measure of all things.

###

Universal Public Domain

THE BATTLE OF ISSUS
Mosaic, From the House of the Faun, Pompey, 1c BCE

Key battle at hand:
immortals vs men,
emperor against boy-king.

Darius, in golden chariot, looks in disbelief:
*Fate cannot be in her right senses to send
a teenager to menace my divine presence!*
Alexander, on his Bucephalus,
as on the pinnacle of a star,
is aiming his eye's spear at an idea:
*Heaven cannot brook two suns,
nor earth - two masters!*

Darius – covered to his eyes,
has hurled his immortal glance

against the boy's advance.
Alexander – without helmet,
hair ruffling hostile air, face enchanted:
wanted to be recognized by them all –
man, wind, animal, sky, earth –
all were welcomed to meet
Alexander-to-be-Great

His eyes piercing ahead,
but not on the emperor,
not on his army pushing the horizon,
not on the spears slicing the clouds,
but on the vanishing point
of his last and only doubt.

History versus eternity.
History – old, experienced, skilled.
Eternity – young, untamed, inflamed.
While Darius drowns in the beardless boy's gaze
Alexander is kissing eternity's eyes...

###

Universal Public Domain

FAMILY VISIT
Doni Tondo, Michelangelo, Italy, 1506

At last, with the Holy Family,
but first, one has to pass
the renaissance x ray test:
primal light slicing draperies,
carving shades, blinding eyes.

Retina recovers, but I struggle to pass
the mind–blinding test –
the Virgin snuggling
between her old man's legs;
I beg for a solar eclipse,
but the sun never sets
over the genius's stance
on the Renaissance mysteries
of holy romance.

Their hands circle around the holy child

like birds shielding the nest
from unseen ominous chase.
O, how Michelangelo enshrines all visions
in this lofty orbit, but closes the entry
to the child's divine sight –
he is playing hide and seek with the rays –
little eyelids vaulting them from eternity
into his mother's doting look –
tying the knot of infinite suspense;
while his vivacious limbs kick away
the last compositional hints
and researchers now can't decide
if he is suspended to the mother
or haled up to the father.

It is both –
just 33 years apart.

###

Universal Public Domain

RISING
Master of Trebon, Resurrection Panel, Prague, c. 1380s

It is a red sky, bloody red;
derived from it a triumphal mantle
wraps the divine sense in scarlet
underlined with palm green;
the stars are gold-made –
their hue – quarried from his halo;
the Golgotha rocks are muted dark –
theirs is a ghostly deadly mark,
but now cancelled by his rising:
he - stepping over its obsolete lid,
cross in hand, bestowing blessing
and taking that larger-than-life gait
that only a novice toddler does
and a god on the rise.

The artist, the master of Trebon,

must have yearned badly for benediction
as he placed the divine
on his own focal point,
unlike others where he stirs up,
dashes above, or stands jubilant
on the high grave plinth.

This rising, so down to earth,
let the painter's pained heart
lean symmetrically upfront
unto Jesus' open wound
imparting thus the mortal love
on the right perspective;
he – remaining on this milestone,
holding tight his live-reddening brush.

###

Universal Public Domain

MONA LISA
Leonardo Da Vinci, Italy, 1503-1514

Mona Lisa,
what belief did you use
to keep your look so unused?
What feeling toned
so smoothly your appearing?
What thought crossed your mind
when Da Vinci brought musicians
to incite your smiling mission?
What silk was your dress
to make your body timeless?
What revelation stirred
your eyes, hands, stature, whims
in this nutshell of a poise?
And finally,
what believable mystery
did you do

to smile it off your life
into our unbelievable drive
to you, Mona Lisa?

###

Universal Public Domain

LUCREZIA AS POETRY
Salvator Rosa, Florence, c 1641

Made of silk, milk and a pinch of salt –
her hair craft is the trophy of the temple
veiling the release of a turn of phrase –
when and how is the muse's choice;
spilling locks as slant rhymes
pin epic genre with a warming tenor;
spiky anaphoric implications
tune to wake up muted contemplations;
weighty layers of allusions dust
metaphoric sense to wounded dreams.
Liberation streams.
Blade brows guard
the dictum of her eye pact:
"nothing but the naked truth"!
Her feather quill is an old angelic relic
for trailing iconicity of fairy making

and though the scriber is withdrawn,
the vellum fulfilled, the volume closed,
a starry gist is about to twist out of her lips
and crown this floating vision
without utterance or change of countenance.

###

Universal Public Domain

ARTEMISIA'S SELF-PORTRAIT AS THE ALLEGORY OF PAINTING
Artemisia Gentileschi, Italy, 1639

You aren't interested in our coming,
you are torn between a double streaming
leaning to us, flying to the canvas,
deriving your features for another image –
Artemisia – you are in allegorical labor –
you stretch from immanent to imminent,
sleeves' frills flapping back and forth
into the obscure allegoric well,
suspended high enough to propel
the brush into mimetic harvest
and just about deep to scoop
profound spirit for your parabolic being.

Your delivery has been long coming –
the first allegorical birth by an owner

of real births – five, to be precise,
this – emerging before our eyes,
your breathing - deep and fast,
we, the believers in a twin world,
set to embrace it with a double love.

But how to abstract the allegorical
from the real? Your eyes deny a clue –
they are hooked unto the brush
pulling the concept's umbilical cord;
lips closing in a unifying motif
of eternal silence and first utterance;
hair in loose bun trying to herd
lost hues and ambient light;
dress laced as an earnest perception
lined with cathartic palpitations.

You recede into your offspring
and with the final push
of breath and brush
this pertinent nativity of art
reels onto the canvas
bundled in Caravaggist shades,
but the first cry of the newborn
with its instinctive urgent grip
seized the finger guiding the brush
and drew it afloat the tenebrous surge.

###

Universal Public Domain

THE MODEL'S REST
Jose Ferraz de Almeida Junior, Brazil, 1882

The model raises her hands
to cease the moment
golden cover falls to the ground,
unbound her arms spread
over the piano like wings,
fingers lure and fold bright tones
by three by ten by fifteen – diamonds,
her naked body shrouding.
Opposite, the ruffled old notation book
as an abbess of this cloister
with her staled creased habit
confronts the dexterous revealed novice.
The melody cascades, the notes tumble
bright and breezy. She sways
a capriccio coda. He claps.
His gallant countenance

embraces her nude performance,
but his teeth chock behind the cigarette
the ornament of the moment:
the notation abbess
opening her wrinkled habit by rote
tricked the nude –
she played the same tune
romped here all the time by everyone,
so he didn't rise to sacrifice
his mundane smoky habit.

###

Universal Public Domain

PRIMAVERA
Sandro Botticelli, Italy, 1482

You must be madly in love
to enter this maze of shaky shades
to meet a deity at human pace.
Such is Botticelli's mediation between
heart's desires and their divine mentors.

Come, it is just the right time –
Mars is here, but not fighting, nor philandering;
Cupid is aiming, but hasn't sent his arrow yet.
They have gathered for the gala of rebirth,
now just opening the gifts they brought.

Look at the orange tree – it brings bloom
together with his last year fruit!
What an early surreal treat!

See Chloris, the flower goddess,
she is fleeing Zephyrus' abduction,
her hands stretched in distress,
as she enters the canvas without vestment,
but full with the spirit
for the earth's entire foliage.
Heroine's test.

The three graces have arrived
to adorn the soul of rebirth
with Joy, Chastity and Beauty
clasping hands with sacred grace
along the bonding string of all beings,
here wiring in their little palms.
Handmade holiness.

Venus is blessing the scene with loving divinity,
while her lover is jetting away suspicious clouds,
as her naughty son is aiming his arrow at Chastity
trying to undo his mother's perpetuation
of the Platonic ideals of the ancients.
Manmade contest.

Chastity will soon be hit,
Mars' job – overclouded,
Zephyrus will fully tear Chloris'
green vestment in nine months,
Venus will grow tired of Cupid's darting…

It is clear that you and I have to take
these volatile lines in our hands:
we cannot control our birth,
but we can master our rebirth –
every spring, every morning, every moment.

Primavera is here, now, carpe diem!

Universal Public Domain

MANET'S OLYMPIA
Olympia, Eduard Manet, France, 1863

She is looming over a pivotal moment:
after the flower before the fruit,
waiting for her inner goddess' birth.
A black cat sets Paris at its vintage best,
a bouquet signals that he is on his way,
her eyes contemplate the fate
with ambrosial sway.

But it is a double play.
The role is looming large.
The real model is in charge.
Victorine Meurent – the budding goddess.
Manet's Olympia – the bedding promise.
Oblivious fingers hold on the silk scarf
as partner in dangerous art;
a tight neckband invites a charming hand

to unfold an amorous advent;
behind – a pitch black rebuff –
Olympia before the well of the fall.

Victorine is eyeing the inner call
to save the soul behind the role
sheltered between flower and fruit
as in the void of a flute.

Olympia, when unveiled,
was rejected, scandalized, failed.
Victorine, unseen, went ahead
to advance her tour de force
emerging goddess of creative might
and artist in her own right.

Olympia – object of desire
with a multimillion mystifying glance;
Victorine – subject to her inner
desiring countenance.

###

Universal Public Domain

SUNDAY BEST
Palm Sunday, Victorine Meurent, France, 1880

You are expecting his coming,
celestial air resting on your hair,
a palm branch nestled in your hand –
dressed in your Sunday best
you look ahead trying to see through
the stillness of the mystifying void.
It is going to unfold – just a week;
since you have revised
your hosanna words by heart
and thy heart by thy same words,
the churning trepidation will find its elation.
And the palm branch will lead the way
to that appointed moment when you will see
that the void is nowhere to be seen.

###

Universal Public Domain

LE DEJEUNER SUR L'HERBE
Edouard Manet, Paris, 1863

Brunch on the grass – scandal in the Salon.
Fair enough – it was the first free-born.
The outlaw, in her original natural glow,
beams accompanied by invisible nymphs.
The hosts, in sober jackets, cravats,
beards and hats are locked
behind an endless verbose fence.
Scandalous, indeed...

They will stay chat-stuck, transience-packed
until you stop seeing them as you cease believing them.

The bather, emerging from the water,
is a feather lost in the wandering 'libre verse'.

The odalisque, in her nude magnitude,

sets an essential turn of phrase:
her eyes, cast out of the canvas
are descending on the approaching, charming beau
with expressive unshielded alter ego…

###

Universal Public Domain

THE POTATO EATERS
Vincent Van Gogh, Holland, 1885

April 1885, Nuenen, Netherlands.
Dark interior. Stillness. No romance.
Dinner. Potatoes. No pies.
A meagre light curbs a scanty catch in the air –
the old man's white cup extended to the old lady in black;
tending the tea, she doesn't see this chance
of mutual ambiance.
The denial continues with the young couple –
the man's gaze is sent away
from the lady's imploring eyes on the side.
The young diner's back entirely declines
a sight into her plight.

Van Gogh has denied any sparkle of bonding
between equals in longing. Here is
the peasants' plain existential account –

the daily expenditure of muscle and mind
to the last blow of strength and command.

Their potatoes are set on the table in good order,
the light reverberates on their peeled orbits
and evaporates with the steam, leaving a lonely
unnoticed gleam - they are to replenish, not to enjoy.
Vincent's peasant, at the table as in the field
is a sole warrior of strife, in life's knot's tightest bent,
 with no victory at hand – nature's hazardous decoy,
 the dark side of the pastoral ploy.

Grumpy faces: smiles – snatched by the wind.
Battered hands: cuddles - burned by the sun.
Ruffled bodies: costumed joy - washed away by the rain.
Rough attitude: fine manners – buried in the soil.
Vincent's peasant – the liberator of the earth apple
from the underground's dark grapple.

###

Universal Public Domain

STARRY NIGHT
Vincent Van Gogh, France, 1889

It's last call:
Vincent brushes the hills' tresses,
blows out the village candles,
appoints the night watch –
a tough cypress comrade –
and only then aims for the stars.

His brush swirls in the thick of night
– a thief's key in a prison lock
to unchain the celestial sea.
Blazing blue and liquid gold
sea gods lunging headlong –
claws keen, tails mean,
they gulp down the nocturnal mesh
and splash trying to reach Vincent's shore.
A honeyed moon leads the tune

and holds this enterprise together,
though its tides shift as we speak,
we can see stars breathe,
the night watch is fast asleep.

###

Universal Public Domain

PICASSO'S SCREAM
Guernica, Pablo Picasso, Spain, 1937

"Nobody leaves Picasso"
he shouted after his last lover,
when she went away forever.

Indeed, it is illusion to leave the draw
of the besotted brush that found
tinted whiff in angular format –
it pins unto the mind's raft,
its sharpness cutting the tides
of the swelling ocean of poise.

When I reached his painted scream –
the grey, groaning Guernica, it was surrounded
by school children, big group, they stood
in front of it, their uniformed ginger tops
retracting flaming shades on Guernica's
fragmented world:
their silence guarding its toll,
Guernica unfolding to children man's fall.

Behind the children's reactions
Guernica was reproduced
into even more fractions:
a shadow of a shivering hair
 disjoining a cut limb,
a girl covering her eyes
doubling a bodiless head,
a boy shutting his ears in palms
scattering to all sides the deafening cry
of the woman with the lifeless child.
World, are you listening?!
The pain so close, children
are multiplying the loss.

Some were trying to put on paper
what they could see through tears
and trembling fingers.
One girl penciled only a cross.
Nobody leaves.
Everyone remains with a piece of soul –
a candle to Picasso's Guernica of the world.

###

Universal Public Domain

ENNUI
Walter Sickert, Britain, 1914

To be in a dream or not to be in a nightmare –
that is the conjugal questionnaire.

This obtuse sitting, this adrift stare,
this blunt contra-poise
to her cornered despair,
it all seems beyond care…
Yet, her chocolate skirt tilted to share
the space and tone of his brown wear,
but it is a futile pursuit,
it is a cul-de-sac route…

The objects do not object, they react:
the table is vaulting headlong
and by the end of his drink

will reach the chest of her support
and discharge its stuffy load:
the bulging knobs already eyeing
to pin the shady crawling...

The stranded associates will then pair
to be framed for posterity's welfare –
the degree of his obtuse entitlement
will mirthlessly overlap
her entanglement –
a back-to-back oblique drive
drawn from mid-to-late life...

"But it started as a high fly"
says the witness from the wall –
a dreamy youth looking forward
to become a prince' charming sweetheart,
her excitement spilling out of the canvas
to sail to the future and steer
romancing feel and flesh
to a consort ever after fresh...

O, this angelic nuptial flower,
now hushed motionless
under an obtusely streaming
sub-consciousness:
a mirage
drained into
a nightmare,
the border crossed
with nothing to declare –
a phenomenally poor,
filthy rich thoroughfare

where
even cigars
cannot respire…
###

Curtesy to the artist

TWO WAY TRIP
Light Gently Leaving, William Stein, UK, 2018

This is a meta-trip – mind's drizzling descent in time of light's gentle ascent.
From the celestial pediment the mind enjoys the sky's soft cloudy crown, reveres the world's primal configuration, and high-spirited jumps unto the seventh formation. Engulfed in soothing sensation it meets Venus on the road to the Platonic world; sees the ascending light sifting translucent presents along the way; the mind bends and picks one — it opens by touch, it is a beam - and while the heart is sinking in its hollow might, the mind is beaming into a luminous meaning of itself. Ways of blooming.
Alone, I reach the working pitch – two perfect orbits; here light throbs shape and time into an ideal form – infinity, as the astro-dynamical orbital rotation turns time reversal – eternal. So, all you need is a circle? But how you put in motion such supreme mission?

By omission – I watch closely: how weightless the hand that sets the priceless orbital cargo on the tiny tip of the conical iceberg; how mighty the sense that coheres in reverse measures; how stirring the spirit of this solemn congregation: I feel my sunken heart rising to the horizon of this luminous junction and catching a glimpse of the beholding phantoms – the lightness of the light, the shapeness of the shape – the Platonic eidos – boundless…the mind, out of itself, drizzling – *the leaving – endless…*
On the side, only now I note the orbits that contemplate the thrill, keeping their cool; the mind again – *they chronicle that way…*
Mission encircled.

###

Universal Public Domain

WHAT IS IN A NAME
Love, Robert Indiana, USA, 1970

Small – one syllable, but impregnable as citadel,
breath-taker as phenomenon,
but risky as pronouncement – built with
lateral approximant, rolling hole and voiced fricative –
how to shelter in such unsteady edifice –
you may slip, sink, or get caught in the friction.
Some never try. Many give up. A few stay.

Robert Indiana's brainchild
brought a radical rebirth.
He changed the mode –
he raised it stand on its feet,
no more a small walk in the park,
now – a tower – one has to learn
the grammar rules of hiking:
not only how to breathe in high altitude,

but how the significance is born
out of climbing the meaning.

Look how the silent "E" saves the falling "O",
it happens, no? Three measures of sound
backed by one of silence – golden mean? - perhaps,
 or – the acting nirvana of Robert Indiana.
Its colours strong and clear – grass, fire and sky –
growing, burning and shine,
no manoeuvrings in undertones and hues:
thus, he let it tower as a phantom flower
up between skyscrapers,
down on alleys, among crowds,
before, above and beyond all doubts.

Many climbed the structure
over and over again to find out
what is in the name.
Indiana's is an upbeat cue:
it's up to you -
to flap its resonating wings
as close as lips as far as stars…
…to a perfect mess…
…or imperfect bliss…
…or anything missed…

This global drama was honoured
in 1973 with a post stamp
for the value of 8 cent.
Affordable. Transportable. Deflation.
Post-lost in towering transactions.
###

Curtesy to the artist

THE ARTISTS' BALL
Tchavdar Nikolov, Bulgaria, 2017

It has been their dream:
to meet for once all together to share
their artistic flair not in reflections
but in real joie de vivre affections.

The party is in full swing – the 12 o'clock
chimes are echoing in Veronese's lute,
Matisse, centre stage, dancing wild
for a bet with Toulouse Lautrec,
whilst Renoir is tangoing his advance
with romantic grace;
Picasso, bewildered, his Chanel stripes
out of tune with his cubist mind, but behind,
his Demoiselles d'Avignon together with
Modigliani's girl loving the fun.
Someone is not impressed – Gala,

like Siberian gale sinking Dali
in her feet and in his disbelief
of reality's vigorous expressions he thought
he had buried under his surreal compressions.

Come the royal entourage, Da Vinci,
Michelangelo and Rembrandt,
balcony rightly reserved for their high verve,
and though what they see is away of their legacy,
like all royals they never complain,
they never explain...even smiles...

Near, Botticelli is helping debutant Venus
to come down and be introduced
to her peers, but Cézanne and partner
have blocked the way to the three exotic girls
entertained by their artists –
the Master, Degas and Gauguin.

In all this vim and vigor you may discern
the old biblical vein – *vanity*,
but now we enter the presence of one
who never dipped his brush in its rush –
Vincent Van Gogh – sat down, in the corner,
 ear cut, he is cold – all his fire donated
to potato eaters, postmen, doctors, sunflowers,
stars – Van Gogh as his own saintly mirage.

This lofty low spot is challenged at a tangent
by the top charmer, Raphael,
his crafty cupids waiting for a sign to strike
whoever's heart he deemed right
and the plot is hatched – Manet,
the Salon's rebel, upgrading his model

from the green grass to the Folies Bergere
white tablecloth and offering her a glass –
alas, she doesn't care, she is searching
outside the canvas for the real treasure.

Wanted – Liberty, the eternal call,
bigger than life, bigger than fame,
leading the big world with the little boy
with bigger than him armament.

###

PART 2
SCULPTURE

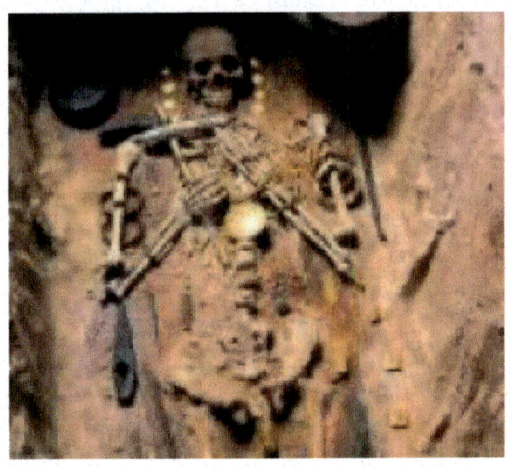

By the kind permission of Varna Regional Museum of History

THE FIRST GOLD
Varna Necropolis, Thracian, 4,400 BCE

He can't rise and show us the glory
of his golden story - he is bone, he is skeleton.
But we can bend over his golden horde
and ponder and count its fragments –
as man does with gold;
but they are so many, so shiny,
they will mess our mind –
as gold does with man.

Come and see for yourself -

a man, clad in six and a half kilograms
of gold bits of mysterious shape and form,
which survived him with six and a half millennia,
is a singular scenery – all had a purpose, a task,
even his phallus was enthroned in golden casket.
Now they are a mass with a message masked,
but not lost. Let's pose.

You can guess by his bone –
he was tall, bold and handsome
like everyone's role model;
he laboured, battled and hoped
like all of us in tough times;
but unlike most of us - he prayed
persistently and passionately to his sun god;
god and gold captured his mind –
their unchangeable shine molding a belief
that both are of the same kind.
The fact is – the sun, with the neutron star,
fathers the gold.
This priestly golden horde was his totemic post
for his god that the message had been got.

And it went in wide circulation –
 golden apples, means, hearts,
and other gold standards.
One of them was buried in the seventies.
The old belief is - when alarmed
the deceased turn in their grave.
The fact is – this gilded man emerged from his
Chalcolithic necropolis on the Black Sea shore,
when the global gold standard was made redundant.

Now, before museum's opening hour,

you can discern his silhouette
under the shine of his solar mantle
by the gilded Black Sea waters
as his god fills his sarcophagus
until they drown in each one
under a single golden rule:
gold is for ritual, not for riches!
###

THE FIRST ART
Cave Lascaux, France, Paleolithic

The Bulls' Hall is man's first space designed to impress. The Black Cow welcomes the guest to a reception for thousands where you meet with horse, rhino, bison, unicorn, feline – strolling from side to ceiling, some displaying a feeling like the horse greeting you threshing his mane.
This is a prelude to the showcase in the Shaft – a buffalo knocking down a bird-headed ithyphallic man. Surely, a convoluted encounter as a rhino is deserting the scene, while the horse has distanced himself on the opposite screen.
Was this the Neanderthal's fall? Under his blunt circadian depression and bitter plants consumption he would have come here weary, hair disheveled, face bashing behind the first bird he caught after long surveying stunned its flair gliding the air. He would have felt bewildered servant of a wonder.
Or the Homo Sapiens' initiation brawl? Under the smart click of his brainy pitch he would have come here to declare a new dominion share with his first catch of a flying creature,

assuming control over its face. He would have felt a master of a new equation in the world of wild contention.

Or the buffalo's fury against the flying being, taking the human attention in a territory impossible for his earthy convention?

The birth of an infinite dream – the conquering of the sky.

The drama is caught in the middle of the bout and the fate of Icarus' precursor may never be discovered.

He will forever remain in his ithyphallic pain…and this notifies a representational miss – there must have been an object of desire in the mist, a woman who stirred him into fire. He hadn't seen her for long, lost in bird hunting, now finding himself in libidinous flame he was running to her and was near when the bull appeared. He was about to touch her…but to no avail…there was no one to help.

Just she…she alone with the loss…then, suddenly – in unchartered trance – grabbing the charcoal and saving her man on this wall of pain! A stick man? – after life the ultimate sign – stick, bone. A bird head ? – the subliminal sign – the spirit – now bird, flown. She with the holy point.

The art beyond which all is decadence,
as by Picasso's stance!

###

By the kind permission of the Ancient Museum Nessebar

AMAZONOMACHI
Lekythos with Relief, Thracian, 4 c BCE

This merciless whiteness –
stomping the eye, just as
some two millennia ago
it smothered the black clay
with the scorch of the fight,
burning in heretic verse,
which to this day
doesn't let the phantom away.

The clash is fast and ferocious,
this protruding twisted leg just rushed in
to unleash its spell; was delayed
preparing the paste of chalk, milk
and pearl for this memorial.

Is it a ritual combat, or a fight

for fight's sake, or a nemesis' contest?
Truth is – she is here to battle to the death
semi naked unprotected
shielded armed man
she had the night before in her bed.
This creamy body, these flying breasts,
these playful legs he was caressing last night.

Why the fight?!
For their survival bet:
love *without* falling in love!
Measured, cut, lived – one moon, one love,
one man – thrown in the morning
in his ship or sea, as it happens.
One hand fighting for love
the other – against falling in love.
A hard spell.

But it rings a bell:
modern experiments affirm
that the body's chemical emission
when falling in love is the same as
the one released when in viral infection.
The monster is duly named Interferon!
And, note, it's true for women, but,
quote: *"not necessarily for men"*!

You guessed it long, long time ago!
Amazonians, how did you catch the
picky cunning ghost and put a bridle
to its neck where so many choked?
Penthesilea, you fought the harshest
battle of all – the Trojan war –
you wrestled Achilles with bare hands,

tell me – which one was harder to prevent:
the fall of Troy or the fall in love?
Hippolyta, your tight girdle was a hurdle
for Hercules' hand – can you swear
that you didn't fancy him at all?
Otrera, the first Amazonian queen,
how did you govern fire within?

You didn't leave memos,
just wondrous demos.
Now that the fight is closed,
the monster – exposed,
time is to give it a second chance –
to infinite advance.
But first you have to fall in love
with the falling in love,
and only then the interferon
can take it from you to the unknown
keeping it real within the ominous surreal...
This is the right fight, yes, curious –
we are on the same page, Amazonians –
warriors of the measures of all heart's whims
before the interferon-less man became
the measure of all things...

###

By the kind permission of the National Archaeological Museum Bulgarian Academy of Sciences

THE LION'S SHARE
Lukovit Treasure, Thracian, 4 c BCE.

It is drama's strangest puzzle –
the animals' king running for his life –
compressed in every sense, the lion
can't believe this man-controlled
fellow horse's aggression, he isn't
versed in animal-man coalitions.
His last gaze strikes: "Brother,
this is unfair, I invented *the lion's share*" …

Was this deadly grip a creative quantum leap –
a tamed stallion defeating a famed predator;
hasn't the sculptor overused his artistic licence
to enhance the master's greatness?
So, who is the master?

History is silent, but the craft is eloquent:

drama in stirring action, proportion,
décor and sense – the rider is surely
somebody of high fame:
skilled, confident, alert –
this isn't the local shepherd,
randomly abandoning herd for game –
this is a trained skill, motivated will;
this is a bravery bill.

At that moment all eyes were set
on the rising star of a Macedonian boy,
tutored by Aristotle,
and on his first action in Thrace.
In this teenage lad – classic profile,
fair complexion, firm determination,
you can recognize the nature and stature
of Alexander from the Battle of Issus.
His marked Bucephalus right here,
both loving lion-hunting so much so –
Plutarch cared to note that Alexander
was a member of a lion-hunting squad.

We are facing the coming on stage
of the charmer of history –
Alexander the Great
in his first formal advent,
a real and symbolic affair,
getting from Thrace his lion's share
before he left on his never-to-return
campaign to the world's eastern end.
His lion's share still growing strong
east, west and beyond...

###

By the kind permission of the National Archaeological Museum Bulgarian Academy of Sciences

SILVER GILT RELIEF
Lukovit treasure, Thracian, 4 c BCE

Stop, please!
Let her go - she is heavenly,
she is the love of the world!
Let her free – don't blood your beauty too–
this kingly spirit, those golden tresses!
Stop – this is the shortest cut
from predator to saviour.
It is the right moment – it is poignant,
behind your closed eyes you are exalted,
but in this split moment
there is a split feeling to your ambiance –
you are not devouring,
you are captivated, mesmerized,
you are more of a lover than killer –
in a way she is the victor here –

hope she can hear this silver gilt justness
of my painful ekphrasis
in these split reflections
of this ever-splitting
silver sans gilt
deconstruction.

###

XXXXXX

SHINING
Seikilos Epitaph, Tombstone, Greek, 1c AD

You stand still and introduce
yourself by the book:
"I am a tombstone, an image".
You point that *"Seikilos placed you here"* –
it weighs, most forget the helping hand.
Then you reveal your mission –
"sign for everlasting remembrance".
This equates to Sisyphus' chores –
you are to push your own stone, sign!
You then show your heart line:
"While you live, shine"!
O, sign, you are rising from the tomb!
Your bearers, the laborious letters,
winged and shooed like Pegasus,
in perfect column they canter ahead
through stone and time and human neglect,

I can hear their pointed shoes
chiseling your breast, their bony wings
darting your flesh to deliver the deathless news.

And they surpass:
behind the candles
their slender silhouettes
dislodge innocent steps
and smoothly set foot
unto the flickering field –
they steer, lean, shine –
the image has risen, I am stoned…
I hear my voice from afar:
"I am an awe-stone, an image,
my breathless heart glued me here –
letters, you can step on it, and we will
shine in one vision…nearer and nearer…"

###

*By the kind permission of the National Archaeological
Museum Bulgarian Academy of Sciences*

THE THREE THRACIAN GRACES
Stone Relief, Thracian, 2 c AD

We bathed in the nymph's spring,
scented our skin with wild rose petals,
draped our scarves over the shoulders
and came to the forest for the dance –
the daily prayer to our sky god.
It is our familial art – we sing and dance
what we draw from the celestial
syncopation and weave into our vital drive.
The scarf is the totem of our craft;
we always keep it in hand, high,
it should never be dropped on the ground
this is a bad omen – for a sky fall –
our only fear in the entire universal ordeal.
Now, since you know the secret,
let's honour the sky dancing its way:

move your waist like cloud waves,
rise hands and scarf like sun rays,
keep thigh upon thigh
vaulting like the moon,
let your feet dart the earth
by the throbbing of the heart
and look up to the sky to grasp
the rhythm of the shooting stars…
O, the milky cluster is out – we have to go.

You fare well along the weaving trail!
We have to move heaven,
without budging the sky!

###

Universal Public Domain

LION IN WAITING
Knidos Lion, Hellenistic, 3 c BCE

Recumbent, six-tone large,
brother by marble of the Parthenon,
as the same quarry bestowed your stone,
you are enormous, you are colossus.
But you are not ominous–
your head is turned aside –
away is the dream of your heart.

You were born on balmy seashore,
you guarded a famed tomb,
you commanded splendid sea views,
your days were bathed in sun rays,
your sleep folded in starry shades,
you were in your colossal elements.
You still looked aside.

Now your eyes are deep set –
retina shrunk in constant alert,
irises faded in imagined pursuit –
they still search –
relentless but not merciless,
restrained but not inert
committed but not anxious –
your waiting, filled with our millions
adoring glances, has permeated
your soul and tuned
your colossal passion
to its divine proportion:
you are now a marvel
overlooking a marvelling horizon;
such accord brings only wonders –
so, it is a matter of time
when your heart's dream will come
as you have imagined, from aside,
and then your flanked look
will beam at her eyes exactly right.

###

Universal Public Domain

FALLEN ANGEL
Auguste Rodin, France, 1900

I've fallen down. I am a fossil now.
Back – plunged with swishing sound.
Limbs – twisted around body bounds.
Wings – missing in action.
Head – in impulsive retraction
 as if to tell how I fell…

…As angels do –
I was guarding a hero
fighting for a good cause –
the loyalty pact of word and fact
His nemesis - the twister,
was targeting his every step.
His deadly word
hissed between my feathers
and hit the hero's heart.

He was slain at once.
I missed my guarding chance.

The hero didn't beg, he didn't cry,
he sang the truth and bid me kiss-goodbye.
I took his soul and tried to fly.
But the soul refused to leave the hero behind –
I had to abide, so we three grappled
to flock together and I took off
overloaded and in raw weather…

…In mid ether my wings went off…
Instantly I was falling.
My companions – speedily down-rolling.
I saw the hero catching my wings
and the soul scrolling around him –
from afar it looked like a dance
of some unknown provenance.
Suddenly we exchanged roles –
they – guarding my safety,
I – relying on their advance!

The hero landed first as a defusing mat,
spreading my wings as a big hug;
the soul - kneeling and nesting a soft cuddle,
and, finally, I – falling in the middle.

This is my fall's history.
The rest is biblical mystery.

###

Universal Public Domain

CHRISTO'S PONT NEUF
Christo and Jeanne-Claude, Paris, 1985

I am a Pont, Pont Neuf,
Now I am an oxymoron –
the oldest of them all.
I watched them grow and take
all the kisses, proposals, and vows,
leaving for me only memories.

Until my vanguard rebirth
as a Pont Wrapped –
a child of Christo and Jeanne-Claude,
when three million pairs of eyes
came to see me in my bundled disguise –
I was beaming like sunrise even at night,
the Seine was mirroring faithfully my joy,
we lured back all the kisses, vows and proposals,
of all lovers, dreamers and puritans,

even the future of their memories.

As that ancient king in a baking clime
who covered his garden mount with white silk
to create the illusion of a snow...
The power of the glow...

###

Universal Public Domain

STONY WONDERS
Michelangelo Buonarroti, David, Florence, 1501-1504

1. Faith wonder
*...He chose five smooth stones from the stream,
put them in the pouch of his shepherd's bag
and, with his sling in his hand,
approached the Philistine...*
While the shield-less shepherd
was facing the giant of muscle and arm,
at heart he was standing
before the giant of spirit
who set in his hand the right stone
for his mission ahead.
And the pebble was towered straight
to its target.
2. Art wonder
He chose from the fate stream
one refused redundant chunk

to give it a second chance.
He chiseled with light beams
its blind cold flakes
to open the eyes,
to untangle the curls,
to galvanize body and limbs
and liberate from the marble
the hidden marvel –
the shepherd of stones.

3. Life wonder

...The stone which the builders rejected
the same is become the head of the corner
...and it is marvelous in our eye...
A flake of faith less in David's
or Michelangelo's hand
and it would have been a giant miss
for the stones and for us.
Faith, the art of life, lights up the night
shepherding the master's carved rite:
Dear to me is sleep:
still more, being made of stone...

PART 3
NOTES AND NARRATIVES

THE SLAVE POET
Hymn to Helios, Mesomedes of Crete, 2 c AD

Emperor's slave, sun's friend –
that is a turbulent poetic wonder
to be handled safely by bound hands.
Will you make it, Mesomedes?
Chained to the imperial domain,
touching the celestial realm –
it reads as an inscription on thin air:
formal capitals upon private cursives –
two bells clashing
to conceive the voice of your measure.
And it is a treasure.
If you were able, while making your master's endless
breakfast, to see that
the Sun begets the lovely day with the flowing rivers of his deathless fire,
then your soul was not in bondage.
If you could sense, while cutting marble for your master's
tomb, that
the Sun's benevolent mind rejoices while it whirls around the manifold raiment of the Universe,
then your heart was not enslaved.
If you could hear while guarding your master's earth
shaking snores
the leisured song of the stars upon Apollo's lyre,
then your spirit was never a servant.

By the same token, in reverse, your master's enslaving knack was affirmed…or annulled…but that only you knew…
###

ANTIGONE

Antigone, Sophocles, Greece, 441 BCE
Performance at Odeon of Herodes Atticus, 10 July 2018

Sat on a stone from the time she was born,
I wait for Antigone to take her place
on the same stage, below the Parthenon,
under a waning Gemini moon.
She enters: her step – silent,
her dress – pallid, stature – moonlike,
receding in the columns behind.
Rises her voice – not a staged flow,
neither a classic oration,
but a fractured cadence of carved sounds –
cracked pieces flash in the night,
chip in each other's path,
sound and echo sparring and soaring,
a surging resonance that dismantles
the heartless noise of the epoch
to carve the sister's love's epos
under the sanctuary of the Acropolis –
at points sharp like its pediment,
at points bold like its columns,
at points sunken like its lost mass,
but towering above mortal law
to immortal outcome – death,
a victory of a sister's loving heart;
its only edict – a tear – I swear –
it made a golden cut in the flow of time,
lit a corner in the motionless divine
and with its sublime ascendancy
re-composed the solemn mass
of the methodical skeleton of the Parthenon.

###

ROYAL MANUSCRIPT
The Gospels of Tsar Ivan Alexander, Bulgaria, 1356

Bright crimson leather over old wooden board;
pearls, precious stones, diamonds – lost;
revelations, miracles, hope, love –unharmed –
a travelling teacher across time and space,
tutoring tsars, princesses, monks, scribes,
kids on fathers' shoulders and on trees
to be able better to see – you can meet them
all inside, many times, welcomed by
the tsar and family standing in pomp,
but what is the circumstance?
Let's go along the trodden lines:
the words, scribed by blessing hand,
stay calm, their meaning – young;
between them the images open and close
like praying eyelids – hundreds of times
to disclose the uncreated light
for you to see, if you deeply wish.
And the circumstance unfolds –
see how the lines make space
for the real king – the king of kings,
look how he teaches –
with eyes and book and grace and gestures –
leaning mercifully over his subjects –
regality coming of age,
the circumstance.
At the end you will learn by heart
the silent prayer – at the time they were
deeply versed in the Hesychia,
so nothing could be lost in translation,
or transliteration, or transubstantiation –
it is the daily immortality here,
the bread that is in the prayer.
###

THE FIFTH SYMPHONY
Ludwig Van Beethoven, Vienna
Premiere conducted by Beethoven 22 .12. 1808

The Fate knocks on the door.
Four fists in revolt strike
the never-before-nor-after.
The door crumbles beneath itself
with no way to resurface
just as the Trojan gate.
Beethoven *grasps fate by the throat,*
as he meant, to unleash the Fifth
element – another door opens –
that of the Trojan horse –
and a legion of soldiering sounds
storm everything within their orbicular
bounds, but echoing in Beethoven's ear
as a faraway rage from Homer's page.
The quintessence in obverse revenge
between loud throat and muted ear;
the fate fights to find its own pier;
the Fifth triumphs to the last note
 of this quintessential premiere.

But Beethoven continues to conduct
and there are no more notes to direct,
 the Fifth is plummeting
over the bare cliffs of his ear,
until someone dares
to turn him to the clapping hands.
And the Fifth bows to his laurelled notes.
And Beethoven stands still not to crush them
beneath his crucified hearing.

###

TOCCATA AND FUGUE IN D MINOR
Johan Sebastian Bach, Germany, 1708

The keynotes unlock the cells' code
throwing the key beneath the stave...
Inhaling freedom, they jump
on the ladder of elation
swiftly to cascade down,
nearly avoiding stampede of sub-fugue-tion...
...freedom's intoxication...
Composing themselves again,
to heaven, they propel,
feet - pedaling the hell
sweeping every evil spell
in every little cell. The air bends
under the voluminous timbral stead.
The mind fights to reflect.
The soul is out of breath.
...The code is being reset...
Each note is now a supernova
letting virgin heartbeats to take over.
Toccata and Fugue in D minor.
A major existential diviner.
###

PART 4
TEA OR COFFEE?

DARJEELING
It isn't a word it isn't a naming,
it is a mystery of sonic making,
acoustic brewing, sound incarnating.
The first syllable darts through the dark
and stamps the bottom of the cup,
the second beams at the sun
and resonates within the walls,
the third illumines the surface -
the champagne of teas
streams in sparkling phonemes -
strong consonants hug trembling leaves,
bright vowels respire colour and scent,
finally all kneeling in meditative gleaming;
the sun is rising over Bengal mountain -
a dream of darjeeling the living.

###

THE OLD CAFE

It has travelled a long way,
crossed many a borderline
to reach this isolated morning on time.
I welcome it with fresh water and sweet
and offer it the fiery spot;
it begins whispering its story of old times:
of goats going mad after tasting its beans,
of birds alerting mystics
to its enigmatic bitterness,
of songs farmers sang at harvesting
of shooting stars falling in its blossoms
sighting now under its silky veil,
which at that moment is torn in pieces
and the starry spirit blooms to reveal
the symphony of its 800 aromatics.
800 smooth conquerors capture the air,
the day breathes their jubilation
in a cup of coffee of old times
sat by a suspended isolation.

Index

PART 1 – PAINTING	9
THE RECLINING REBEL	9
THE MEASURE	11
THE BATTLE OF ISSUS	14
FAMILY VISIT	16
RISING	18
MONA LISA	20
LUCREZIA AS POETRY	22
ARTEMISIA'S SELF-PORTRAIT AS THE ALLEGORY OF PAINTING	24
THE MODEL'S REST	26
PRIMAVERA	28
MANET'S OLYMPIA	31
SUNDAY BEST	33
LE DEJEUNER SUR L'HERBE	34
THE POTATO EATERS	36
STARRY NIGHT	38
PICASSO'S SCREAM	40
ENNUI	42
TWO WAY TRIP	45
WHAT IS IN A NAME	47
THE ARTISTS' BALL	49
PART 2 – SCULPTURE	52
THE FIRST GOLD	52
THE FIRST ART	55
AMAZONOMACHI	57
THE LION'S SHARE	60
SILVER GILT RELIEF	62
SHINING	64
THE THREE THRACIAN GRACES	66
LION IN WAITING	68
FALLEN ANGEL	70

CHRISTO'S PONT NEUF	72
STONY WONDERS	74
PART 3 – NOTES AND NARRATIVES	76
THE SLAVE POET	76
ANTIGONE	78
ROYAL MANUSCRIPT	79
THE FIFTH SYMPHONY	80
TOCCATA AND FUGUE IN D MINOR	81
PART 4 – TEA OR COFFEE?	82
DARJEELING	82
THE OLD CAFE	83

Printed by Printforce, United Kingdom